Patriotic Songs

When Johnny Comes Marching Home

A Song About a Soldier's Return

Written by Patrick S. Gilmore
Edited by Ann Owen • Illustrated by Todd Ouren

Music Adviser: Peter Mercer-Taylor, Ph.D.
Associate Professor of Musicology, University of Minnesota, Minneapolis

Reading Adviser: Susan Kesselring, M.A., Literacy Educator
Rosemount-Apple Valley-Eagan (Minnesota) School District

PICTURE WINDOW BOOKS
Minneapolis, Minnesota

Patriotic Songs series editor: Sara E. Hoffmann
Musical arrangement: Elizabeth Temple
Designer: John Moldstad
Page production: Picture Window Books
The illustrations in this book were prepared digitally.

Printed in the United States of America.
1 2 3 4 5 6 08 07 06 05 04 03

Picture Window Books
5115 Excelsior Boulevard
Suite 232
Minneapolis, MN 55416
1-877-845-8392
www.picturewindowbooks.com

Library of Congress Cataloging-in-Publication Data
Gilmore, P. S. (Patrick Sarsfield), 1829-1892.
  When Johnny comes marching home / by Patrick S. Gilmore ;
edited by Ann Owen ; illustrated by Todd Ouren.
  p. cm. — (Patriotic songs)
Includes index.
ISBN 1-4048-0171-5
  1. Patriotic music—United States—History and criticism—Juvenile literature.
  2. United States—History—Civil War, 1861-1865—Songs and music—History and criticism—Juvenile literature. 3. Children's songs—Texts. [1. United States—History—Civil War, 1861-1865—Songs and music. 2. Songs.] I. Owen, Ann, 1953- II. Ouren, Todd, ill. III. Title. IV. Series.
ML3551.4 .G45 2003
782.42'1599'0973—dc21
                                                    2002155005

O say, can you hear America singing?

America's patriotic songs are a record of the country's history.

Many of these songs were written when the United States was young.

Some songs were inspired by war and some by thoughts of peace and freedom.

They all reflect the country's spirit and dreams.

Get ready for the jubilee!

When Johnny comes marching home again,
hurrah, hurrah!

We'll give him a hearty welcome then,
hurrah, hurrah!

The men will cheer and the boys will shout,
the ladies they will all turn out,
and we'll all be there
when Johnny comes marching home.

The old church bell will peal with joy,
hurrah, hurrah!

To welcome home our darling boy,
hurrah, hurrah!

The village lads and lassies say
with roses they will strew the way,

14

and we'll all be there
when Johnny comes marching home.

Get ready for the jubilee,
hurrah, hurrah!

We'll give the hero three times three,
hurrah, hurrah!

The laurel wreath is ready now
to place upon his loyal brow,
and we'll all be there
when Johnny comes marching home.

21

When Johnny Comes Marching Home

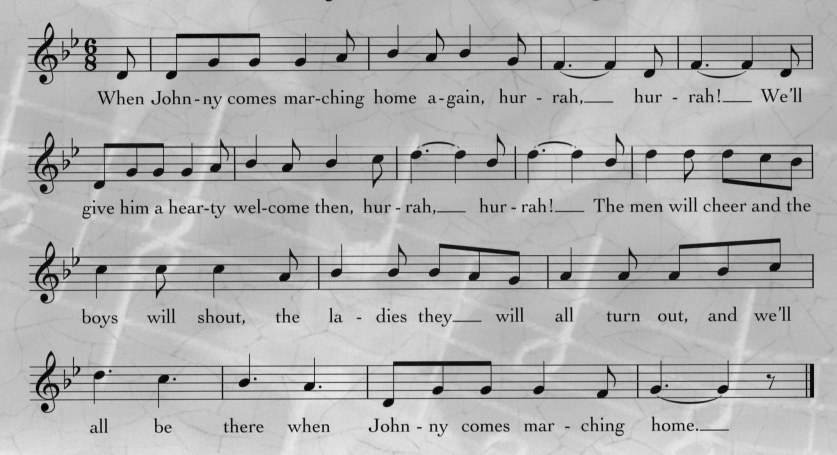

When John-ny comes mar-ching home a-gain, hur - rah,___ hur - rah!___ We'll

give him a hear-ty wel-come then, hur - rah,___ hur - rah!___ The men will cheer and the

boys will shout, the la - dies they___ will all turn out, and we'll

all be there when John - ny comes mar - ching home.___

The old church bell will peal with joy,
Hurrah, hurrah!
To welcome home our darling boy,
Hurrah, hurrah!
The village lads and lassies say
With roses they will strew the way,
And we'll all be there
When Johnny comes marching home.

Get ready for the jubilee,
Hurrah, hurrah!
We'll give the hero three times three,
Hurrah, hurrah!
The laurel wreath is ready now
To place upon his loyal brow,
And we'll all be there
When Johnny comes marching home.

About the Song

"When Johnny Comes Marching Home" was written by Patrick S. Gilmore. Patrick was the leader of the Union Army band during the Civil War (1861-1865). Patrick was born in Ireland in 1829. He came to America in 1848 and settled in Boston. Soon he was known as a great musician and bandleader. When the Civil War began, his band often played at rallies and military events.

During the war Patrick wrote many marching songs. "When Johnny Comes Marching Home" is the most famous.

"When Johnny Comes Marching Home" is about the excitement people felt when soldiers came home after the war. Some people think Patrick borrowed the tune to the song. It may have come from an Irish tune that warns about the dangers of war. Other people say the song was taken from an African-American spiritual. Today, "When Johnny Comes Marching Home" is one of the best-known songs from the time of the Civil War.

You Can Make Johnnycakes

Civil War soldiers didn't have ovens for baking bread. Instead, they would make their bread in a skillet. Johnnycakes are a type of cornbread cooked in a skillet, like pancakes.

What you need:

1 cup (237 ml) water

1½ cups (355 g) ground yellow cornmeal

½ teaspoon (2 g) salt

½ cup (118 ml) milk

oil or butter for greasing skillet

An adult to help you

What to do:

1. Make sure you have an adult to help you.
2. Bring the water to a boil in a saucepan.
3. Mix the cornmeal, salt, and milk in a bowl.
4. Carefully add the boiling water. Stir.
5. Melt the butter in a skillet over medium heat.
6. Drop spoonfuls of batter into the skillet, leaving room between each.
7. Cook about 3 minutes on the first side and about 2½ minutes on the second until lightly browned.
8. Serve with butter and syrup, or your favorite pancake topping.

To Learn More

At the Library
Bunting, Eve. *The Blue and the Gray.* New York: Scholastic, 2001.

Lyon, George Ella. *Cecil's Story.* New York: Orchard Books, 1991.

Raatma, Lucia. *Patriotism.* Mankato, Minn.: Bridgestone Books, 2000.

Ransom, Candice F. *The Promise Quilt.* New York: Walker and Co., 1999.

Turner, Ann Warren. *Drummer Boy: Marching to the Civil War.* New York: HarperCollins, 1998.

On the Web
FirstGov for Kids
http://www.kids.gov
For fun links and information about the United States and its government

National Institute of Environmental Health Sciences Kids' Page: Patriotic Songs
http://www.niehs.nih.gov/kids/musicpatriot.htm
For lyrics and music to your favorite patriotic songs

Want to learn more about patriotic songs?
Visit FACT HOUND at http://www.facthound.com.